Introduction

I started working with Path Breaker Pastors in 1990. I served as a denominational overseer of 60 churches and could pick out the 12 that were turning little into much. They were leading the way.

My mentor Lyle Schaller then helped connect me to Leadership Network, an organization that only focused on innovators and pathbreaker pastors from across the US.

These pathbreaking and revolutionary pastors were often founders, launching their churches with little more than vision and grit. Alternatively, they had taken over the leadership of a smaller church that had now grown very large under their leadership. The system looked to them to provide vision and direction, including their legacy season.

Everything had changed under their leadership.

The Leadership Network staff told me: "We think pastor succession will be a big issue in the future. Start working on it."

That began my journey in speaking with these larger church pastors, convening workshops with people like Lyle Schaller, Peter Drucker, William Bridges, and Jim Collins to talk with groups of pastors about the issue and learn from them.

In 2002, many of those pastors began calling me to help their boards do similar thinking. As in all "boomer things," they were reinventing the legacy season for their generation and beyond.

Those consultations led to more consultations, workshops, and some preliminary processes. By 2012, I had become the CEO of Leadership Network with little time to engage with these great pastors and their churches, but the demand was

33 Basic Statements on Senior Pastor Succession

Healthy Endings to New Beginnings

BY
Dave Travis

Printed in the United States of America.

First Printing: January 2024

ISBN: 979-8-218-34925-7

still there. Since 2010 through workshops, groups, and individual coaching conversations, I have spoken with over 500 senior pastors and churches, and over 5000 engaged in the process of transition.

These include several groups: Those that are passing the baton, those that received the baton, and those that passed the baton some years back. Each group holds a piece of the relevant story.

To address the issue productively, I designed better tools and processes. I have become a consistent guide to walk beside the pathbreaker pastors and their leadership teams to ensure their succession process went well.

In 2018, I retired from Leadership Network to give my full attention to consulting with churches in this area.

We developed the Senior Pastor Smart Succession Process and now have coached many churches through this critical season.

The following few pages describe some basic statements and facts that every church should know, even those we don't help.

At the end, we will point you to some other helps and resources to give you some guidance but know you can always call us for a free consultation conversation to help you get started on your unique journey.

PS. The "33" is an homage to my late, great friend, Lyle Schaller, who wrote multiple books with "44" in the title. I am about ¾ as good as Lyle, so I kept it to the best 33.

1. The Larger and Longer, the more intentional the process

Elephants are the largest land mammals. Their pregnancy period is twenty-two months.

On the other hand, rabbits can go from conception to birth in around 28 days.

In my work with large churches, they tend to be more like elephants.

The larger the church and the longer the senior pastor has been there, the more critical it is to have a very intentional succession process. It needs good thinking and process.

Invariably in my opening conversations with a church, they will describe complications "unique to our situation." Rarely are they unique if you work with over 200 churches, but they are unique to them.

Complexity and complications mean there needs to be a customized pathway that fits your church, not someone else.

(You will want to see our Senior Pastor Succession Process Model to understand fully)

2. Founders and Near Founders add another layer of getting it right.

There was a great wave of churches starting from 1980 to the early 2000s. Praise God for that.

Many of these leaders are true founders, the initial pastor that stepped out with vision and faith and built a large congregation around their gifts.

Now many of those that are the founders are retiring or stepping out of primary leadership.

Near founders are those transformational leaders that may not have technically been the founder, but the church was transformed during the season they have led. Often that meant a relocation, a name change, a significant model change, or multiple changes of the preceding items.

In addition, over 85% of the congregation has never known another pastor at this church other than the current pastor.

Here is what I find:

- Founders are more likely to stay around after stepping down as primary leaders. That role needs careful crafting, guardrails, and clear understanding, but most can do so with sound guidance.
- Each year you stay over 20 years as the primary leader also makes staying more likely and needed, even if you are not the founder. Again, this can work with proper help.
- Honored successors with fewer than 15 years in the role are likelier to leave any future role. There are a few, but it is much rarer.

Which are you?

(These issues are addressed in the Leader's Future part of our process)

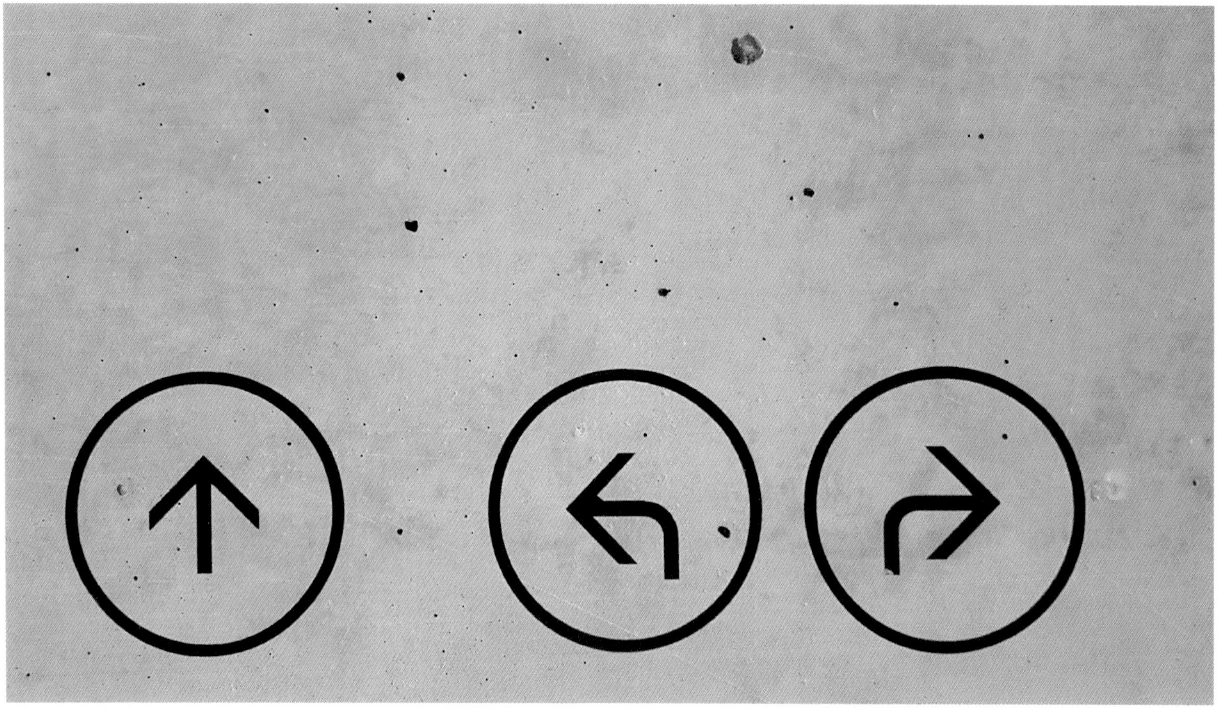

3. The ultimate goal is the long-term health of the church. That is the client.

As leaders, thinking of our own needs and desires is natural. But we all realize the more important desire is to see the church flourish even more in its next season.

It is not wrong to think of the current leader's needs and to give special consideration to their ongoing relationship with the church and its mission.

But we must align what we want for the church's next season and what serves it best for that season.

In the Senior Pastor Smart Succession Process, we take the time to differentiate all constituencies' various needs and desires and craft a plan to maximize the best outcomes available.

The two extremes we want to avoid:

- Total focus on the next leader's needs and desires without regard to the rest of the church.
- Letting the current leader dictate what they want and how the next season will create a tribute to them.

Those are obvious and meant to be funny. But you would be surprised how many church teams tend to err towards one of those extremes.

Staff and Boards can either be very loyal toward the current leader on one extreme or resentful on the other.

We need to recognize that the church's health is influenced by intangibles that include honor and respect of leaders but also set a direction towards better health.

(This is addressed with our Purposeful Plan Framework in our process)

4. Succession is the *intentional* transfer of power, leadership, and authority from one leader to another.

This was my definition long ago that my friends Dr. Warren Bird and William Vanderbloemen used in their excellent book, *NEXT*. (Don't worry, they gave me credit.)

First, it is intentional. We develop a plan and work out our plan. Sure, there may be bumps, sidetracks, and slight diversions. But we define where we want to go and the general plan that gets us there.

Second, it transfers power. Power is the ability to direct work to others on the team. The primary leader of a church should have much of that power, or it should flow through their office to appropriate team members.

Third, it transfers leadership. Leadership influences the whole system through relationships, teaching, coaching, and motivation toward our end goals and visions. In a church context, it is the right to cast the vision for the whole system.

Finally, it includes the authority its governing system granted to the lead pastor to make certain decisions to exercise the power it grants. In some cases, that authority is derived from the congregation. In other cases, the board or denomination. It is often also found in the governing documents.

We run into severe complications when we neglect to transfer all of those things to the new leader.

(This is addressed in our Paced Pastoral Plan in our process)

5. This is the guiding compass point question: What does success look like three years after the handoff?

Most churches focus on finding the next leader. I suggest you know the outcomes you want AFTER three years as a better starting point.

Defining success measures for:

- Current leader and family
- Next leader and family
- Board
- Staff
- Congregation

It is a process that builds towards alignment. We define those directions tangibly (what) and intangibly (the feeling we want). The clearer the outcomes desired, the better the chances of success.

This helps all the parties build toward that end. It allows us to define what type of leader we need next. It helps us give that leader a clear direction of where God would have us go as a congregation.

Often in this process, I have to help teams come to a sense of reality around expectations, but defining them lets the whole team know where we feel we will go in the next three years. A part of this process is deciding how much continuity or discontinuity is desired. Generally, continuity is desired if things look good in a congregation. If the last few years have been rocky, some discontinuity in direction is sought. Whatever is decided must be communicated well to the candidate, board, staff, and congregation.

This is often missed, and the next leader leads in a different direction than the congregation expects. That leads to miscommunication, distractions, and division.

(This is addressed in The Futurestory Brief in our process.)

6. *Kairos and Chronos*

Chronos time is calendar time. We measure it in days, months, and years.

Kairos time is God's timing. When the New Testament talks about time, it focuses on a season of God's outpouring. Sometimes that is NOW, and sometimes a future season.

"Now is the day of salvation" or "for in due season we will see the harvest."

Many pastors begin thinking in this way with Chronos time.

"I will turn 65 in October of 2025." Or "How many months should this take?" Or, "How many months between my announcement and the new pastor's arrival?"

These are good questions. But also consider Kairos time.

When is the best season momentum-wise for the change in leadership? What is a good marker for the church and congregation seasonally for a change?

In the U.S., 65 has some mythical properties that pastors consider. Primarily, it is about Medicare health benefits.

This should not be a hindrance to handing over primary leadership though.

My comeback is usually: "What if you could continue in a role with these benefits when you are 60?

Would that be better for the church?"

Once that conversation begins, pastors begin to see great possibilities.

(This is a part of the Robust Readiness understanding in our process.)

7. When the student is ready, the teacher will appear.

That saying – the attribution disputed among scholars of various philosophies – does describe what I see in pastors.

They must be ready to engage in these serious conversations about their future, their family's future, and the church's future.

When they are ready, the process goes smoothly.

Wise pastors call me when they start thinking about how to help the church in this transition. That is an excellent sign of readiness.

I often receive calls from patient staff members of a large church asking about their senior pastor: "How can we encourage them their time is up?"

Or, more kindly from a board member: "We want our pastor to leave with their head held high. How can we start this process?"

I give them a few suggestions but then quote that opening line. I even have a readiness tool for pastors that helps them determine their abilities to lean into the conversations.

(This is a part of The Strength Framework in our process.)

8. Their spouse must be ready as well.

Most of the senior pastors I have worked with are male. I have worked with one or two females Senior Pastors as well.

Regardless, their marital partner also has to be ready for this process. The spouse is often ignored in the process. This is a big mistake.

I once spoke with a staff member whom the board had charged with researching "best practices" in succession planning. Their wise pastor had initiated the conversations with the board but felt they needed some guidance.

"Has the board asked the pastor's wife how they feel about the process?" The staff member stuttered with an answer: "I don't think we have talked to her at all."

"Have her come to the next meeting and ask her," I replied.

They followed that advice. Later their testimony, both in audio recordings and written communications, explained that when asked, she began to weep and replied: "No one has ever asked me about major decisions like this that will impact our marriage and family."

I have learned that before starting with any client, I want to interview the spouse first to gauge their readiness to enter the conversation. I want to hear their needs, desires, their point of view about their spouse's readiness.

Many senior pastors will tell me: "My spouse is ready and will follow me in anything."

I always respond: "I am sure that is true, but I want to hear it myself."

Sometimes there is a surprise in that spouse interview.

(This is also a part of The Robust Readiness part of the process.)

9. *You can walk and chew gum at the same time, but it is hard to walk, chew gum, and juggle running chainsaws simultaneously.*

My experience is that large churches can undertake two major change initiatives at one time, but they can't do three. Small churches can do one at a time.

What is a significant change initiative? An initiative where more than 50% of the staff is involved or more than 33% of the congregation.

These would include:

- A major generosity initiative
- Staff restructuring
- A change in the small group approach or model
- Adding a worship service
- Adding a site
- Changing the Church Management System software
- A succession planning effort

You get to choose up to TWO at one given period. You can do some sequentially but not simultaneously.

Note the last one. This is one that a church reading this book will engage in. Which other one will be happening during that season?

Choose it wisely.

(This is addressed in the Paced Pastor Plan in our framework)

10. Succession is different than search.

"I must find the next leader before deciding on timing."

"We will get started once I bring in someone and test them for a season."

"We will hire a search firm to find a potential candidate, then get started."

(Actual paraphrase of statements made to me by potential clients.)

Succession success begins with the current leader rather than the next leader. That is true even when a church has an excellent internal candidate.

When the focus is on the next leader, you miss key elements along the way that will enable the next leader to be their most successful.

If you start at the wrong place, you might still end up well, but it will generally take longer and be more complicated. It leads to suboptimal outcomes.

It can be compared to a trapeze athlete trying to hang on to both bars for a bit too long. If there isn't a net, that could end up in pain.

Start on the issues with the current leader and help them and the core team through the initial stages.

There is much to do first in helping identify the needs of the next leader to lead the next season at a specific church. We will get to that.

(Much of this happens in the Leader's Future area of our process)

Crayola
Crayola
Crayola.com
Crayola

11. Even Doctors don't remove their own appendix.

Many pastors try and plan their own succession process. But it is hard to balance your needs, interests, health, and the church's health when you try to do this yourself.

Forming an internal team helps. It can give you counsel and guidance.

Depending on your polity, your board should also be an asset in the planning.

But most DIY pastors in large churches try to copy another church's pastor's process, thinking that "we are so much alike." Sometimes, they will even call in that pastor to tell their team how it should be done.

But after working with over 60 churches under contract and counseling another 200 more, I find less in common in these situations than you would think. Even those in the same denominational family or similar governance have vast differences in process and outcomes.

Things can be learned but are harder to apply from church to church.

The tools I use to set up conversations and processes so that each church designs the solution that fits their situation like a surgeon's glove, not a catcher's mitt.

The doctors in my family consult with other doctors and specialists when they have a medical issue, even if it is a common one.

Remember that as you think of whom to call in to help you.

12. As Fred Rogers said, "look for the helpers."

Mr. Rogers said this to children when they felt scared or were in a tight spot.

Another way to say it is "spread the weight out" among different leaders. The decisions in this process need to be spread among several groups to participate in the process that will help bring the congregation along with us through the season.

We form a succession team in half of the consultations with churches I serve.

The others use the board as their succession team. Why do we use succession teams?

Because boards often rotate and change every year. Better to have consistency throughout the whole process.

The succession team can report to the board and have a few joint members, but this gives time and space for thinking, and empowers a small group to do much of the work.

It also takes some pressure off the board. Remember item 5 about walking and chewing gum? Boards have to deal with a variety of issues. This area will take over half of a regular board session at any season.

Finally, it allows input and creativity from long-serving leaders who may not serve on the board or in a search team but have their church's and pastor's best interest in their hearts.

For clients, we have documents that delineate the use of various teams in the total process.

(This is a part of our Productive Pathways area in our process.)

13. Boards need to raise their visibility.

Most of my clients are staff-led. When you get right down to it, they are pastor-led. For those prominent, long-term pastor-led congregations, there is usually high trust in a single leader's direction and competence to drive the church forward.

So, they would say we are either:

- Pastor-led, or
- Staff-led

They would also say they are: Choose one that fits –

- Board
- Elder
- Overseer
- Trustee

And now, choose the next word:

- Accountable
- Protected
- Directed

Or some similar formulation.

So, it could be a Pastor-led, board accountable. Or, Staff led, elder protected. And so forth. But here's the thing – all those words mean different things in different church settings. The roles and responsibilities look different.

Some churches have a group that oversees "spiritual matters" and one for "financial matters." Most congregations have visible boards when there is a crisis. "Our board had to make a hard decision."

It is best to build the visibility of a board in the months leading up to a transition. This helps spread the weight of the congregation's expectations and builds trust among the body during this time.

Don't hide the board under a bushel basket, regardless of how you frame the relationship between pastor and board.

(Your process needs to include governance growth. We use our Generative Governance Pathway in our process.)

14. Do not neglect board succession as well.

In healthy churches, boards are often very stable in their composition.

This is true across almost all denominations. It is true whether the board is large or small. Whether it is a "high expectation" or "lower expectation," this is true.

In some cases, I work with churches that have had the same board members for the entirety of the lead pastor's tenure.

This is not necessarily a bad thing.

But it does hurt your bench strength.

Long-tenured pastors with long-tenured board members, while stable, often need new members as a new pastor takes over leadership.

New board members must be onboarded and tested well during the transition/succession season to do that well.

That change should be a gradual shift, not a total change in one swoop.

How are you training, preparing, developing, and onboarding board members for the future season of the church?

This is a key part of the Pastor Smart Succession Process.

(This is a part of our Generative Governance tool set.)

15. Mind your governing documents.

The governing documents are there for your church for a reason. Too many times, scant attention is paid to them.

While I have seen good governing documents and less than good ones, they are essential to follow lest there be legal challenges.

Two extremes exist in these constitutions, by-laws, and other polity documents regarding succession.

On one extreme are those with stringent requirements for the exact procedure to be followed. Often the document was written or adopted when the church was much smaller, or is required by a denominational body that tends to have many small churches and few large ones.

The other extreme are those hastily written at the formation of the church that has no mention of a vacancy in the lead pastor position. Therefore, there is no guidance in the stated procedure.

In between are those that call for a procedure to be followed, but typically were written for churches that do this more frequently than once a generation.

In my experience, I encourage churches to work within the governing documents or change them ahead of when needed to allow flexibility.

Even within some stringent governing documents, special teams and workarounds can be established that conform legally to the documents, and build a healthier church process.

But they cannot be ignored altogether without the risk of legal challenges in the future.

In the Pastor Smart Succession Process, we do a complete review and check to ensure we abide by the set limits while building a good process that moves the church forward.

(These tools are included in the Guided Growth Pathway part of our process.)

16. Remember the NASCAR Short Track Rule: Go Slow to Go Fast.

There are a variety of tracks on the NASCAR Stock Car Racing circuit. Some are super speedways and intermediate tracks where the driver mashes the gas and rarely touches the brakes. They may slightly let off the accelerator at times, but otherwise, it is all out all the time.

But on short tracks and road courses, rookies must learn that the fastest way around is only sometimes riding the gas pedal. The risks of going off track or hitting a curb will slow the car in a curve that interrupts the car's momentum.

It is better to brake appropriately into a corner so that you may accelerate out of the corner quickly.

While you may slow the car dramatically going into the corner, the total lap time drops when the car can turn gently and then accelerate quicker on the other side.

I remind churches of this when they try to speed through some challenging process parts. It is best to take the time in these corners, so decisions are correctly made, documented, and agreed upon before moving on.

In the Smart Succession Process, we try to move deliberately, not rushed or forced, but not dragging the brakes.

Some churches move faster, and some slower. It depends on the speed of trust in the system and the rate at which key decisions can be made.

Boomer-led churches also find that younger generations desire more input to the process – be that staff of lay engagement. That input process needs time to move the congregation forward together.

(This is part of our process's larger Productive Pathways component.)

Succession Involves Transition

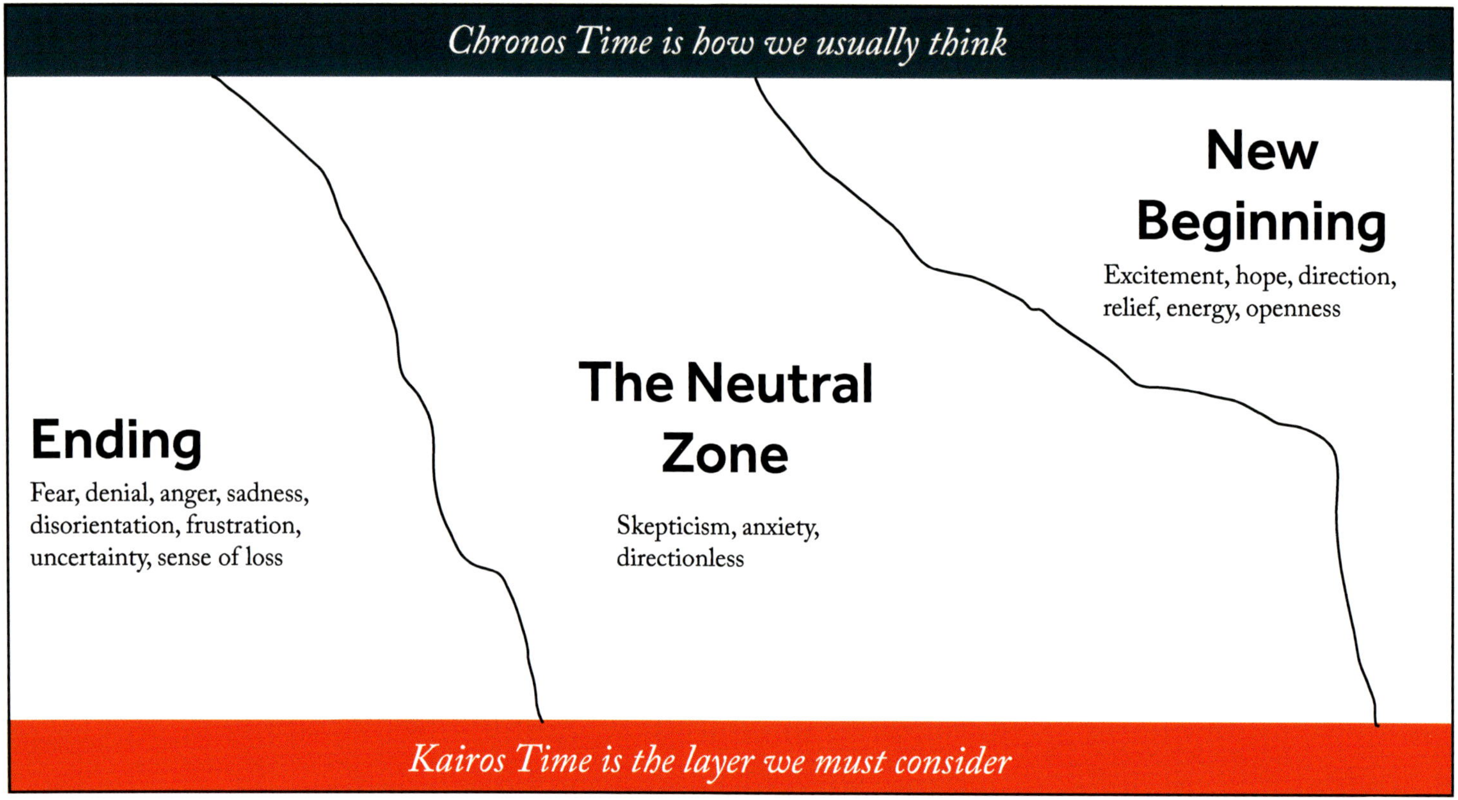

Adapted from William Bridges' 'Transitions for Change Management'

17. Good transitions have healthy endings and productive neutral zones that lead to great new beginnings.

The diagram opposite originated with William Bridges, an organizational change consultant I met with on several occasions.

His theory was that this applied to any significant change initiative. Pastor Succession is one.

His basic statement: "It's not the change that gets you; it's the transition. Transition is the emotion we attach to the change."

Every person in the change process moves through these three zones. There are different emotions in each zone. The timing may look different for individuals, but as a group, one can lead through the first two to set up the potential for great new beginnings.

If we ignore these or speed through them, we are not set up for greatness in the future.

That is why we stage certain communications that roll out over time. That is why in the Pastor Smart Succession Process, we conduct critical exercises over time instead of a tight time frame.

Guiding the system – the current leader, the board, the staff, and the congregation's leadership through these phases builds the base for potential great starts.

We may not get everyone to the new beginning simultaneously, but we can get it within a short season.

We can do this healthily, letting people honestly deal with their emotional losses and anticipate future gains. We must give the first two adequate time and space.

As Bridges wrote: "Neutral zone creativity is the key to turning the transition from a time of breakdown into a time of breakthrough."

(This is included in the Tailored Transition Timeline part of our process.)

18. Succession is a layered process.

Consider the simple table on the opposite page.

Most view it and immediately agree. But many then tend to focus on one of the layers for one of the groups and give light attention to the other layers.

For simplicity, two columns are illustrated – The current pastor and their family and then the rest of the system. Each component of the system should deal with all the layers.

There is a spiritual layer to the process. At this layer, God guides and works on every person's heart, as it can be a season that draws us closer to God and His purposes.

There is an emotional layer. We invest much emotion in our leaders. Leaders invest much of their emotional lives with their congregations. The emotions of the process should not be ignored.

The organizational layer is often most addressed and discussed but is often the most straightforward to navigate. This layer is where most boards, staff, and pastors feel the most competent to discuss, find creative solutions, clarify, and decide.

The other layer is the identity layer. This will be addressed next.

(These issues are related to The Strength Framework and The Purposeful Plan Framework in our process)

Layers	Pastor	Church/Staff/Board
Spiritual	✓	✓
Emotional	✓	✓
Organizational	✓	✓
Personal – Family - Identity	✓	✓

19. Do not neglect the identity layer.

In most of my cases, the lead pastor has been a lead pastor their whole career. In the founder's cases, this person has professionally and personally defined its identity. In some instances, this is the only church they have ever served in any role, with some even growing up as a part of the church before becoming the lead pastor.

In these cases, their identity is wrapped up in being the lead pastor. That mental framework in their head has defined their attitudes and actions.

This is also true of their family. Often a spouse has shared that role identity with them. There are certain deference and unspoken expectations and rewards shared with them.

In some instances, children are also involved in staff or key volunteer roles within the congregation that have ties to the leader, these are respected.

Pastors must reckon with the question: Who am I if I am not the lead pastor here?

Likewise, a part of many congregants' identities is their involvement with this church and this pastor.

You hear it in their language: "I go to Pastor Sherman's church."

This identity change layer cannot be ignored in a healthy process.

(This is addressed in our Leader's Future phase of the process.)

20. The profile you need next is almost always different than the last time.

We work hard to define the profile of the next leader required to lead the next season in the congregation's life.

For current path-breaking pastors, the church looks much different now than it did when they arrived.

The skills and roles required to lead it to the next season are different.

In some cases, the governing documents provide a list of duties often derived from prior generations the next leader is supposed to play.

As a church seeks a new leader, I have seen roles and duties number well above 20 in a job description.

This is a mistake.

With that many roles, no human can perform them all well.

It is better to focus the roles of the large church pastor on certain key areas. Every church can and does look different as to what those areas are though.

I use various tools to help the church focus on the critical roles needed to lead in the next season.

These then inform any development plans, marketing for the role, top grading candidates, interview questions, and expectations for the future season. These will be the roles we measure the next leader on as they lead the church in the future.

(This is addressed in The Power Profile Blueprint.)

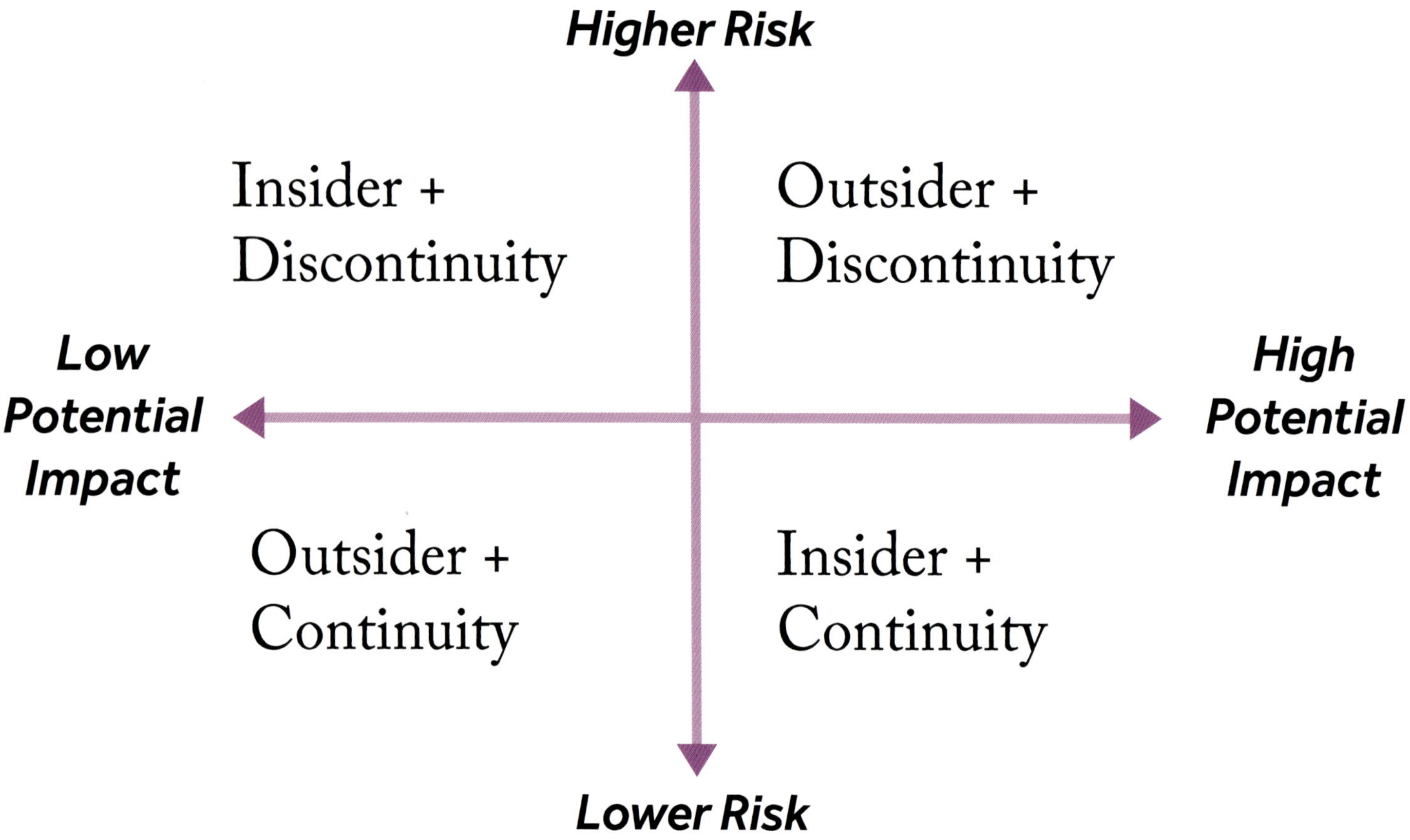
Higher Risk
Insider +
Discontinuity
Outsider +
Discontinuity
Low
Potential
Impact
High
Potential
Impact
Outsider +
Continuity
Insider +
Continuity
Lower Risk

21. The development plan for an internal candidate.

The current board and pastor often see potential in an internal candidate as the next leader.

The diagram opposite shows the generalization of the risks and impact of the potential for internal vs. external candidates.

Unlike many corporate boards, the board of a church rarely has examined an internal candidate thoroughly. Instead, it relies on reports from the current pastor or a few leaders engaged with this leader.

I always recommend a complete development plan based on the expected profile needed for the next leader, conducted in conjunction with the board.

I help design a tool for the evaluation by the whole board, often with a few other staff to give a complete 360-degree evaluation, then a development process over multiple months with a thorough discussion at intervals before making a yes or no decision on the candidate.

This builds not only the confidence of the board in their decision-making about a particular internal candidate, but also builds relationships with the potential new pastor that can help carry the church to a fast start it in its next season.

Those plans should be crafted with care and diligence.

If the candidate is not selected, the board can give commendations to other churches, if desired, about where they feel the candidate is strong and why they were not a fit as the next pastor at their congregation.

If the candidate is selected, the board can honestly say to the church: "We have examined this candidate in every area of their life and feel they are the right choice to lead us in the next season."

(This is a component of the Successor Search process.)

22. Leaders have to lead something.

Leadership is a gift, a passion, a calling, and for some, a natural tendency ingrained in their personality.

For many Senior Pastors, acting as leaders started very early in their life, even before they reached double digits in age. As such, it is tremendously challenging for them to do a total stop from "leadering." (my own word)

Some can find ways to exercise this outside a church within another organization, a club, a community ministry, and the like. With others, we must allow them some measure of leadership within the church for the next short season. This must be carefully crafted and designed. [see item 27 later in this book.]

Others will choose to teach or preach at other churches for at least a short season.

One church told the retiring leader: "We want to continue to pay you to go and minister to other churches and pastors in our region but granting them sabbaticals where you can serve those churches for that sabbatical season for no cost."

Other churches encouraged their pastor: "We know you have a proven track record of helping other churches with your guidance of a network. Let's formalize that leadership role, and we will pay you to do that."

I did have one client some years ago who said: "I want a full stop to ministry. My wife and I will buy an RV and do some travel that we always wanted to do."

Sure enough, they did it.

That lasted about three years. He then took up a series of successful interim pastorates of smaller churches. He couldn't stay away from leading.

Expecting a complete stop for a transformational pastor is an unrealistic expectation.

(This is addressed in the Resourceful Role section of our process)

23. Why do timelines tend to get faster?

This is a reasonably regular conversation with a senior pastor.

"I just turned 55, and I want to begin planning for the season after I turn 65 and turn over leadership to the next leader. What should I be doing now?"

"Why are you waiting so long?" I ask. This then leads to the magic of 65 or some other reasoning.

Sometimes they say: "I need to save extra funds for that next chapter." Or: "I intend to have my successor on my staff for five years."

The conversation changes when I explain the challenges in some of that thinking and then clarify that many pastors can still have a role at the church but not be the primary leader.

The possibilities for leadership and growth begin to multiply.

As leaders get excited about those possibilities, timelines get shorter.

They also begin to understand when I explain the challenges of keeping a great second leader in place for an extended season.

Once a leader and the board understand some of the benefits of changing the "normal" timeline, many opportunities abound.

If you are dreaming of new possibilities now, that could be a sign from God that your next chapter is fast approaching.

24. Communication waves.

Pastors often tell me they want to make a dramatic announcement on a key weekend where they tell "everyone at the same time" about their plans for the next chapter. "I do not want to show favoritism" is the stated reason.

My counsel is different.

Besides working with the board and some senior staff in planning ahead of an announcement, it is wise to bring certain leaders into the process before general announcements to the congregation. These happen in small groupings and individual meetings. Think in terms of waves that grow over time.

Why do we do this?

We do this to get some of the congregation and team a head start on the ending phase of transition. We do this to hear some of the general questions that will be asked that we need answers to give when the full announcement comes. We do this to advise some staff where they will or won't be utilized.

We often give heads-ups to high-impact volunteers and givers, so they aren't surprised when the time arrives. We do this for some founding members and legacy team players with high investment in the current leader.

This often happens within six to eight weeks before "the big reveal," meaning the pastor and their spouse often do many personal meet-ups. It can be very emotionally taxing as well.

I had one client that was heavily small group oriented invite all the small group leaders the Saturday before the congregational announcement to hear the news and the plans.

These growing waves of information allow those that enter the season first to help shepherd others in the initial phases of the process. It also allows the current leader to practice their language and way of telling the story to hone its effectiveness.

(This is covered in our Tailored Transition Timeline.)

LOCAL CALL
CROSLEY
LOCAL CALL
CROSLEY
LOCAL CALL
CROSLEY

25. Make three asks.

This is a companion to number 24.

You should ask three questions whenever we inform the staff, an individual, or a small group about your plans.

Before the general announcement, the ask should include a request to keep this information confidential, as you only tell key insiders before the big reveal weekend.

"Will you pray with me and keep this confidential until (date)?

We should ask them to continue in their service and giving.

"I want to ask you personally to keep your current place of service and financial investment in our church over this season. We depend on people like you. Will you let me know in the next week of your desires there?

We should ask them to support the next leader, whomever it is.

Depending on the person or group you are conversing with, there could be other asks. But make at least three, and be careful of going beyond that. People remember three.

Then ask the person to reach out to you with an answer if they do not give you one. And if you haven't heard from them, call them. Often you will get some good feedback to help you process the transition yourself.

Then when you have the "big reveal," – make three asks of the whole congregation.

They should be similar but more generalized.

Do not miss this opportunity to make big asks for the future health of the church.

(This is carefully scripted in The Tailored Transition Timeline.)

26. Grub the stumps.

One of my mentors grew up on a farm in Missouri during the depression. One of his favorite sayings was, "grub the stumps."

When a field is cleared for new growth and productivity, you must grub those stumps out, so the soil is ready. The stumps can impede new roots that must go down into the ground.

Staff members and critical volunteers have often been very loyal to the current pastor. Some are not bad people, just slightly abrasive, quirky, and cantankerous at times. As another mentor explained: "They leave a wake behind them."

Some of these are personal friends of the pastor they have kept around due to loyalties, past relationships, and even family ties.

But the pastor also knows that the next season would probably be unwise and unhealthy to leave them in their current place of service. This is for those individuals' well-being, the church's situation, and the future leader's ability to lead.

Some of these need to be retired with dignity. Others need to be encouraged to other places of serving.

Some volunteers need to be replaced with new leaders for a season.

Don't leave that to the next leader if you know they are a stump. Have a plan to begin that process before you depart.

(This is a part of Seamless Story section of our process.)

27. Setting up guardrails and referees.

I do this in all my Senior Pastor Smart Succession Plans, regardless of whether the current leader stays in the community.

We agree on clear limits for the current pastor in their next season. This includes a "break" season and a long-term season. Those limits can look different for each of those seasons.

These guardrails also include the church's support for the current pastor in the next season.

We often write these before we have selected the next leader so that we may communicate to them clearly how the former leader will be exemplary and stay out of the way.

We also decide with the board who will be the referee to call the fouls if there are violations in the future.

These are NOT board members. They are not current staff members.

They love the current pastor and the church and can hold those loves in tension. They are often mature former board members with high church trust.

If there is ever an issue with the former pastor violating an agreement or the church not abiding by the support agreements, the person is directed to the referees for consultation and potential correction.

When I establish these with clients, they have never had to be used.

Why? Because things were made clear.

My only disaster was when the board, new pastor, and former pastor decided these were unnecessary for their situation. "We trust each other and know relationships are strong enough to overcome any difficulty."

Let's just say – Trust was broken, relationships destroyed, and total disaster resulted.

(This is part of the Generative Governance Pathway.)

28. Organizations will go as far as their leader is willing to grow and let go.

There is a truism in all organizations.

The leader's growth caps their growth.

In order for most leaders to grow, they have to let go of certain past behaviors and controls.

There were seasons when those controls and behaviors needed to be done by them as the prime leader.

But great leaders have grown where their unique abilities are utilized in the places where they can make the most significant positive contributions. They have learned to let go of the mirage of total control.

The same follows in a succession process.

The sage season enables a leader to use their crystallized intelligence, not fluid intelligence, to give opportunities for others to lead and focus their efforts. And they learn to let go of the system so it can go past their own skills and ability limits.

The scriptures speak of the priests moving from active service to mentoring and instruction at age 50.

In their case, some of that was because of handling the heavy things of God.

Today those heavy things involve oversight of large teams, emotional pain, quality levels, extensive facilities, and significant financial weights.

Great leaders learn to address those but also realize when to release them to others.

(This is a part of the Framed Fit section of our process.)

29. Search Firms and Search Teams

In the last five years, about 80% of my clients have not used the services of a search firm for a senior pastor search.

Do not assume that is the default best answer for a church.

Search firms are a relatively recent tool for senior pastor searches. I have good friends in the business who are true experts. There are some excellent reasons to use them.

At the same time, an internal search team can get the task done well.

They do need the following:

- A diverse set of skills, ages, and tenure with the congregation.
- Time to do the tasks well. This is a longer-term, hard-working assignment.
- Willingness to be "in the middle" between boards, staff, and candidates.
- Wisdom, prayerfulness, and a call from God to serve in this way.

Sometimes, even an excellent internal church search team hires a search firm to do much of the work.

In my client contracts, there is no difference between those that used a search firm and those that did not after a three-year evaluation period. The results were the same.

My experience is that search firms are often blamed for lack of clarity by the board and search team.

Every situation must be evaluated in the light of multiple factors as to whether it is a wise investment to use a search firm.

And it is not the first decision to make. It often should be made in the second stage of the process.

(This is part of our process's larger Future Leader section.)

30. Onboarding is often the most missed item.

Onboarding is when you bring a new team member onto the team and get them started in the right way in the right direction.

This is both a formal and informal process.

But it needs a plan.

After a handoff, countless pastors have told me, "They just sort of threw me in."

Even if the candidate has been with the church in another role, onboarding is needed.

My tool kit has several exercises to help a new leader get oriented to the team and the church's culture and manage the natural expectations that are changing in a new season.

Many first and second-year issues with a new leader can be traced to poor onboarding experiences.

That is not to say that issues still won't arise, but we can avoid some with good onboarding.

(This is a part of our Successor Start Initiative in our process.)

Impact Full

31. Everyone gets freaky about the money, but that is more emotional than reality.

Succession planning takes financial resources to do well.

It's one of those "you can pay now or pay more later" situations.

It is better to dream, design, and spend on the front end than make costly corrections on the back end.

Additionally, many churches assume giving will drop dramatically during the succession process.

So far, I have not had that happen.

Why?

Because we design a process that builds momentum and energy toward the next season in the church's life, and people get excited.

My experience is that many churches can bank additional funds during this season to cover the costs easily.

Hiring a helper like me is a costly undertaking. Often figuring out how to reward the outgoing pastor seems expensive as well. Add in the new pastor's salary, benefits, and moving costs, and it all adds up.

But messing it up can bring worse consequences. Often a 20 to 30 percent drop in giving in some situations and total bankruptcy in others. (None of my clients have had this experience, though.)

This is not the place to cheap out.

32. A plan beats an emergency, but you should have an emergency plan.

Every church needs an emergency succession plan.

An emergency plan is a simple tool that allows the board to immediately name a head of staff or interim leader in case the worst happens.

The board should review it at least once a year.

If you have a big loan balance, your lender often requires this.

Amazingly in at least half the churches I speak with, when asked: “Do you have a clear written emergency plan?”

The answer is: “We have one; it is just not written down.” This is a colossal error.

Or, they will say: “Our governing documents tell us in a pastoral vacancy how we should start the search process.”

That is all good. But a large church will need to move quickly in an emergency by naming a temporary leader to operate day-to-day the many decisions that are made weekly.

Some of the worst disaster stories ever were caused by churches with unwritten understandings, resulting in internal civil wars among families, staff, and boards.

It’s OK to limit that temporary role such as: “The board must approve any staff layoffs or firings during this season.”

The resources section of this booklet will tell you how to get a free template.

And this is true even when calling and employing a brand-new lead pastor. Have a plan that the new pastor knows, and the board knows what would happen. Update it every year.

(This is a part of Generative Governance tool set.)

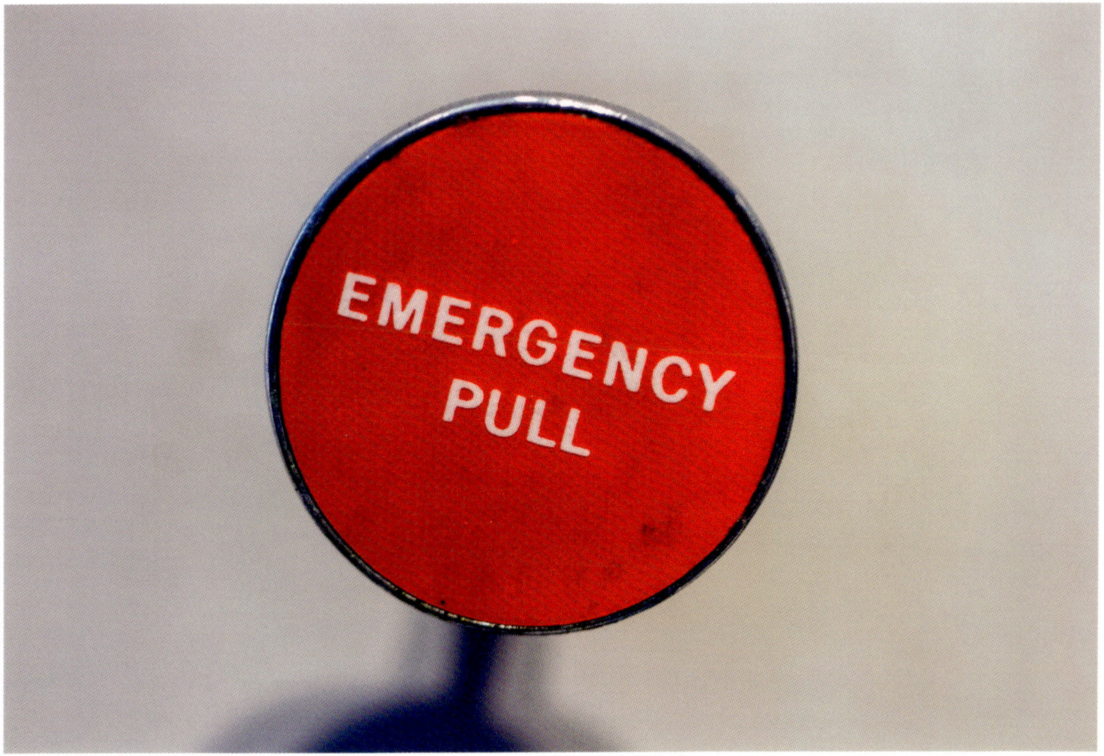
EMERGENCY
PULL

DE L'OUEST

33. Murphy lives.

"Anything that can go wrong will."

There are a thousand ways to mess this up, and new ones seem to be invented daily.

One can't plan all contingencies, but we can avoid the predictable potholes.

One of my early exercises with a group is to have them brainstorm what could happen that would lead to adverse outcomes. It is always good for a laugh but also reminds us that we are all fallible and flawed.

If we identify some trouble spots up front and plan the navigation around them, we have a greater chance of success.

Because this can be a season of high emotion, flaws, mistakes, and small slights are magnified.

Part of my task is to manage that emotional journey and help the pastors and boards avoid the worst disasters.

The picture opposite was a train wreck in Paris over 100 years ago. The commuter train was going too fast into the station. The engineer blamed the brakeman for not applying the brakes soon enough to avoid going through the station. The brakeman blamed the engineer for going too fast in the first place.

Train wrecks still happen and happen for a reason, not randomly. Best to have an intentional plan with safety checks.

Afterword

Throughout this booklet, I have referred to the Senior Pastor Smart Succession Process, our process that helps guide pastors and churches through these seasons.

Our process best works for churches with long-term Senior Pastors that have seen great change over their season in leadership at the church. We call these leaders – Path Breaker Pastors.

Over the last five years, we have seen that our clients experience revivals, and their ministry momentum has multiplied through these seasons of transition and change. Our process includes proprietary tools, plan sheets, videos, and guided coaching to help each church achieve those outcomes.

As you saw on the topic's pages, we alluded to where parts of our process come into play and how it fits together. Our model, illustrated here, captures some of the ideas.

But we would love to walk you through the whole story so you can be better equipped to face this challenge, whether you work with us or not. Even those that see our slides and don't hire us tell us that our concepts and discussions saved them many thousands of dollars and frustration. To schedule that FREE 45-minute mini-consultation, scan the QR code below.

My team includes several experienced professionals that can help you succeed in your succession season. Set up a call today or reach out at dave.travis@generis.com

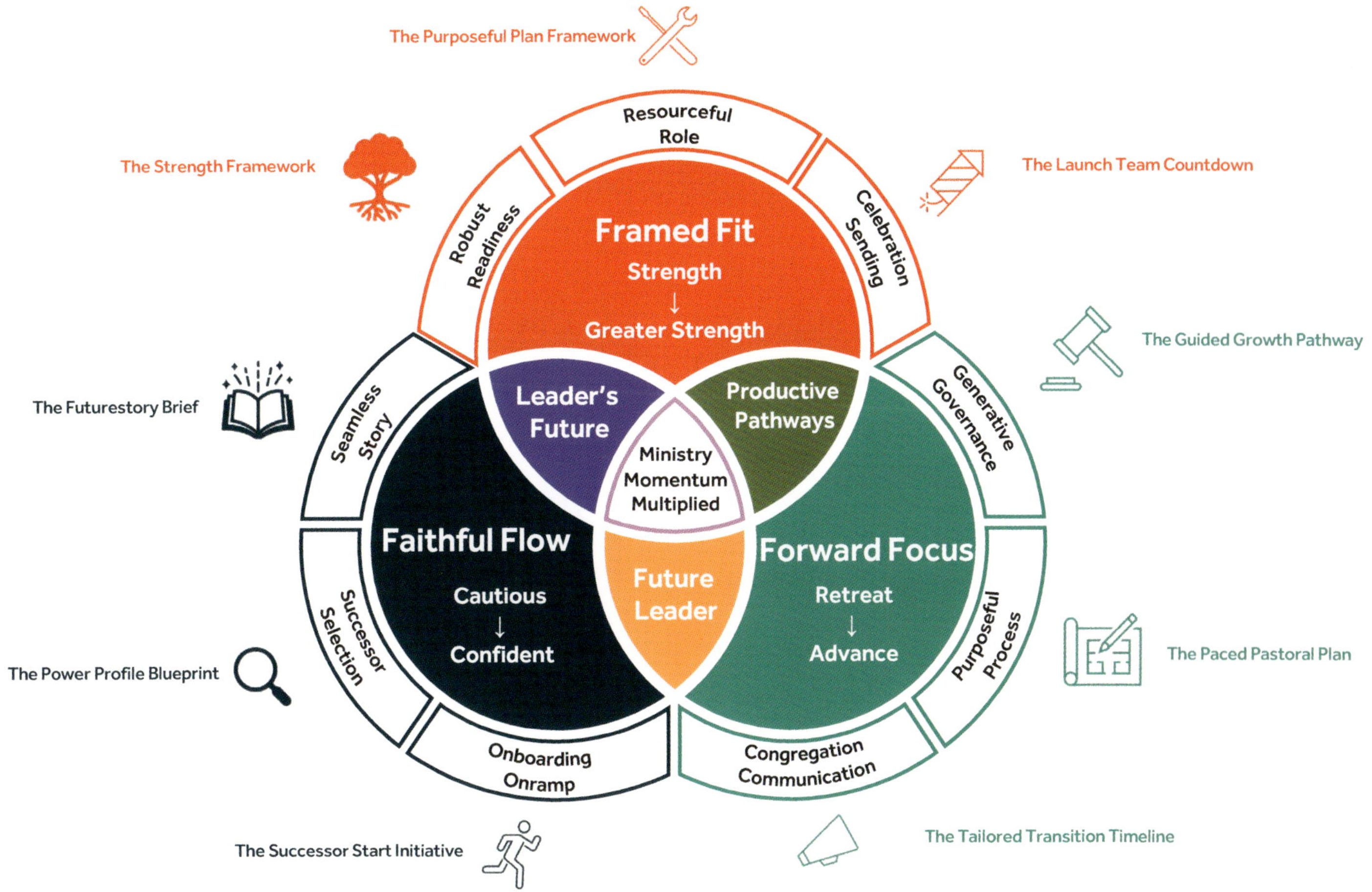

The Purposeful Plan Framework
The Strength Framework
The Launch Team Countdown
Resourceful Role
Robust Readiness
Celebration Sending
Framed Fit
Strength
↓
Greater Strength
The Guided Growth Pathway
The Futurestory Brief
Seamless Story
Leader's Future
Productive Pathways
Generative Governance
Ministry Momentum Multiplied
Faithful Flow
Cautious
↓
Confident
Future Leader
Forward Focus
Retreat
↓
Advance
Successor Selection
Purposeful Process
The Paced Pastoral Plan
The Power Profile Blueprint
Onboarding Onramp
Congregation Communication
The Successor Start Initiative
The Tailored Transition Timeline

Appendix: Image Credits

1. *Photo* by Nam Anh on Unsplash
2. *Photo* by Daniel McCullough on Unsplash
3. *Photo* by marianne bos on Unsplash
4. *Photo* by Matt Duncan on Unsplash
5. *Compass, Aperiodic, From last plane flown by Wiley Post*; National Air and Space Museum; Public domain
6. *Time as Occasion Kairos* by Francesco de Rossi; Public domain
7. *Self Portrait* by Julius Henricus Quinkhard; Public domain
8. *Photo* by Torsten Dederichs on Unsplash
9. *Photo* by Matt Bero on Unsplash
10. *Photo* by Josh Eckstein on Unsplash
11. *The Sick Child* by J Bond Francisco, Smithsonian American Art Museum
12. Fred Rogers, "Mister Rogers' Neighborhood" (circa 1979); PictureLux/The Hollywood Archive/Alamy Stock Photo
13. *Photo* by Zachary Keimig on Unsplash
14. *Photo* by Nastuh Abootalebi
15. *Photo* by Maarten van den Heuvel
16. *Photo* by Tim Trad on Unsplash
17. *Succession Involves Transitions* © Dave Travis
18. *Succession Layers* © Dave Travis
19. *Cake Layers*; generated by DeepAI
20. *Hand Family*, Smithsonian American Art Museum
21. *Insider Outsider Risk* © Dave Travis
22. *Photo* by Thomas Bonometti on Unsplash
23. *Photo* by Jack Anstey on Unsplash
24. *Photo* by Rostyslav Savchyn on Unsplash
25. *Photo* by Pavan Trikutam on Unsplash
26. *Photo* by Rasmus Landgreen on Unsplash
27. *Photo* by Austrian National Library on Unsplash
28. *Photo* by Suzanne D. Williams on Unsplash
29. *Photo* by Matthew Ansley on Unsplash
30. *Photo* by Patrick Perkins on Unsplash
31. *Photo* by Annie Spratt on Unsplash
32. *Photo* by Jason Leung on Unsplash
33. *Montparnasse* Pictorial Press Ltd / Alamy Stock Photo

Afterword: *Senior Pastor Smart Succession* © Dave Travis

Every year I get asked about the succession process that our local church went through. And every time I'm asked to share why it went so well, Dave Travis's name comes up. Dave offered priceless wisdom and a calm presence to help us navigate one of the most delicate seasons in our church's history. We couldn't have had a better person in our corner.

Rich Villodas, Lead Pastor of New Life Fellowship – New York, NY

Dave Travis and the team at Generis brought thoughtful experience and expertise to my pastoral transition from one community to another. Their wisdom and experience prevented many well-intentioned mistakes. Their expertise helped craft a pastoral process for the whole congregation. But their thoughtfulness, in getting to know me, our staff and elders, and both congregations involved is what I will always remember and appreciate most.

Tyler Staton, Lead Pastor of Bridgetown Church – Portland, OR

Dave Travis has been an invaluable resource to our church. His extensive experience in the field of ministry, along with his array of tools and exercises make for an enjoyable partnership. On behalf of myself, our elders and our executive team, we are extremely thankful for Dave and we recommend him to any church looking to grow, restructure or navigate a season of transition.

C.J. Johnson, Senior Pastor at Northview Church - Indianapolis, IN

I'm so grateful that God led us to Generis during our time of pastoral transition. We are facing the future with confidence and clarity thanks to the outstanding and faithful work of our consultant. We couldn't be happier with the results.

Jeff Marian, Former Pastor at Prince of Peace Lutheran Church - Burnsville, MN

Who is this guy, Dave Travis? And why should we trust him to help us in this part of our church's life?

Dave Travis has advised large church pastors for over 30 years.

Twenty-three of those served with Leadership Network, an independent think-tank that served large congregations across the U.S., Canada, and eventually, Europe.

He started as a peon there, charged with doing some research, building the network, and helping figure out how large churches could better do succession. He rose through the ranks, being granted more responsibility in leading the team. He became CEO in 2011.

He decided to retire to get back to serving churches in a hands-on way. He joined Generis in 2018.

Since then, he has worked with dozens of churches and their leaders, helping them solve wicked, sticky challenges through his role as Director of Strategic Counsel to Pastors and Church Boards at Generis.

In addition to degrees from Georgia Tech and The Southern Baptist Theological Seminary, he has certificates and training from Harvard Business School, Wicked Problem-Solving Practitioner from the Project Managers Institute, Million Dollar Consulting with Alan Weiss, Workshop Facilitation with AJ and Smart, and the Association of Conceptual Frameworkers.

In the past five years with Generis, he has worked with over 60 churches and organizations in one of his processes, including Betterman, The Orchard Church, Wheaton Bible, Elmbrook Church, New Life Fellowship Queens, Emotionally Healthy Discipleship, Bridgetown Church, LCBC Church, Eaglebrook, Crosstimbers, Bridgetown Church,

Imago Dei Church, Prince of Peace Lutheran, Christ Fellowship McKinney, Venture Church, Ingleside Baptist and others still in succession processes not yet public.

While Dave brings dozens of tools to each of his processes, the clients report that his most important contribution is facilitating focused conversations to drive change and action. Dave leads from behind or the middle, not putting himself out front, but helping equip and guide the church and organization's leaders to drive the action steps needed to move towards better outcomes and health.

Dave has been married to Lynne since 1985. They have two adult daughters, two sons-in-laws, and a dog.

They live outside Atlanta, GA.

His website is generis.com/dave-travis.

His newsletter is found at https://churchleaderinsider.substack.com/. It's free, but you get what you pay for!